PLANNING
FAMILY
MINISTRY

PLANNING FAMILY MINISTRY

A GUIDE FOR A
TEACHING CHURCH

Joe Leonard, Jr.

Judson Press® Valley Forge

PLANNING FAMILY MINISTRY

Copyright © 1982
Judson Press, Valley Forge, PA 19482-0851

Second Printing, 1984

Unless otherwise indicated, Bible quotations in this volume are from

Today's English Version, the *Good News Bible*—Old Testament: Copyright © American Bible Society, 1976; New Testament: Copyright © American Bible Society 1966, 1971, 1976. Used by permission.

Other quotations of the Bible are from the Revised Standard Version of the Bible copyrighted 1946, 1952 © 1971, 1973 by the Division of Christian Education of the National Council of Churches of Christ in the U.S.A., and used by permission.

Library of Congress Cataloging in Publication Data
Leonard, Joe H.
  Planning family ministry.

Bibliography: p.
  1. Church work with families. I. Title.
BV4438.L46   1982   259   82-12754
ISBN 0-8170-0971-X (pbk.)

The name JUDSON PRESS is registered as a trademark in the U.S. Patent Office. Printed in the U.S.A.   ⊕

Contents

INTRODUCTION

From the beginning of the Christian movement, followers of Jesus have tried to create a distinctive kind of family life that expresses the gospel. In many different cultures and in every historical period, Christians have thought about how to live in families in a Christian way. From the time of the New Testament Epistles to the present, Christians have written tracts, books, letters, and sermons seeking to inspire and guide Christians living in families.

Our time is no exception. There has been an explosion of books on Christian parenting, Christian approaches to sexuality, Christian marriage, and Christian family life. At the same time, secular writers have been busy reassessing the faults and the prospects of family life today.

The purpose of this book is to provide guidance to local church leaders, lay and ordained, who want to develop programs of family ministry. It is meant to be practical and usable in local churches of all sizes. An important assumption that underlies the planning suggestions offered here is that many, perhaps most, local churches will need to cooperate with other congregations and community groups in order to provide the kinds of family ministry programs that are needed. A cooperative approach to family ministry is not a weakness, but a strength. When families in one congregation become acquainted with those in another, they are strengthened in their Christian commitment. When Christian families are made aware of resource persons and groups in the community, the capacity of those families to face difficulties and resolve problems is increased. When churches offer help to families, the opportunities for witness to unchurched households are multiplied.

An important conviction underlying this book is that a Christian family is not an end in itself. A Christian family is a laboratory for producing "citizens of the kingdom." A Christian family is a school where those who acknowledge the sovereign government of God in their lives learn how to apply gospel truths to every dimension of life. A Christian family is a missionary enterprise offering a witness to neighbors, schoolmates, and fellow workers through its way of life. A Christian family does not have to be a helpless bystander observing social change but, rather, should be an engine of social change with the potential for moving a community toward more compassion, more justice, and more health. The goal of Christian family life is not solely to create a family which functions in a healthy manner but also to help the world become a more fit place for the Spirit of God to dwell.

This is work! Families experience success *and* failure. They need support and encouragement, inspiration and instruction, and the assurance of God's grace. Family ministry has an enormous potential for improving the quality of life in individual families, for enriching the life of the local Christian congregation, and for translating the values of the gospel into the life patterns of the community.

Through programs of family ministry, the quality of communication, the depth of mutual appreciation, and the healthy functioning of church-related families can be raised dramatically. New educational methods and resources are available which enable family units to assess their own needs and take action to meet those needs. Marriage enrichment experiences, parent education programs, communication skill training courses, and resources for Christian education in sexuality have been created to help local churches carry out effective family ministry.

Family ministry has enormous potential for enriching the life of a local congregation as well. Of all social institutions, churches alone relate to all generations and all family members. Resources for intergenerational congregational events are widely available and can help a congregation develop a sense of itself as a "family" in which the elderly are respected, youth and children are heard, single persons are included in the circle of caring, and family units are given the support they need to function joyfully.

Finally, family ministry has the potential for mobilizing a congregation as an advocate for family life in the wider community. Congregations with a family consciousness are prophetic voices for social changes beneficial to families in general. No other institution so completely represents families, and no other institution is moved by a richer or more powerful vision of human community. When a congregation takes family life seriously, it will inevitably find itself concerned about the quality of life in the wider community. The strategic role of local congregations is to build bridges with schools, with local employers, with government and labor organizations, with mental health agencies, and with community volunteer groups in order to give voice to the concerns and needs of families. Family ministry challenges a congregation to be the leaven that raises the consciousness of the whole community about the values and possibilities of family life.

CHAPTER 1

The Tasks of Family Ministry

A teaching church nurtures persons in Christian growth. It strives to make each one aware of God's self-disclosure as revealed in Jesus Christ, and it provides opportunities for persons to respond and grow as children of God. A commitment to nurturing persons in Christian growth, then, necessarily means a concern for the quality of life within family units. Family ministry is an essential, ongoing ministry of a teaching church. It is rooted in the needs of people living together; it arises out of a persistent concern that the gospel be lived in our homes and that our marriages, our parent-child relationships, and our decisions about sexuality reflect Christian faith. Because a teaching church has a concern about the wholeness of life and the wholeness of persons, ministering to persons in their family relationships is essential.

Everyone is part of a family in some sense. All of us are daughters or sons; most of us are sisters or brothers, husbands or wives, parents. Some of us are grandparents, aunts, uncles, or cousins. A few of us live in intentional families—groups of persons not necessarily related by blood, marriage, or adoption who covenant together to be a household or neighborhood unit characterized by commitment, caring, mutual support, and sharing. Family ministry is all the efforts of our church to meet us in the context of our family relationships.

Family ministry involves all generations. At one end of the age spectrum, children and youth are candidates for family ministry as they raise questions about sexuality, marriage, and how to get along better with Mom, or Dad, or their brothers and sisters. At the other end of the age spectrum, widows and widowers are candidates for family ministries that will help them deal with grief, aging, and building relationships with "substitute" family members to compensate for the relationships they have lost. The entire church family ministers to itself through events geared to enrich its life together, improve communication skills within it, and relate persons living alone to larger family units.

Family ministry involves mission. Family ministry reaches out to the community when congregations provide opportunities for parent education, marriage enrichment, or family counseling, or make a meeting place available for a single parents group. Family ministry also takes place when church members and congregations enter into dialogue with school systems about the education of children and youth; or work with local industries to create day-care programs near the places where parents work; or become advocates with zoning boards and city councils for group homes, halfway houses, and shelters for the victims of domestic violence.

In sum, family ministry means:
- translating biblical concepts of human relationships into practical patterns for family living;
- responding to the needs of church family members at every point in the life cycle;
- educating and influencing the community toward greater respect for the health and integrity of all families.

THE THREE TASKS OF FAMILY MINISTRY
1. Family Ministry Is an Educational Task

If family ministry is to be seen as an essential and ongoing ministry of a teaching church, it must also be understood as an educational ministry. Family ministry provides families with enriching experiences and practical tools for living. Family ministry is not counseling by another name! Good family-ministry programs provide information and also help families learn the skills of communication and planning they need to prevent problems from becoming crises. Most families most of the time do not need counseling. However, all families at some time can profit from learning more about human development—for example, about how children grow in their ability to make moral decisions. All families at some time can improve their communication skills—for example, how to express negative feelings in a constructive way. Of course, it is important for the church to respond to families in crises. It is equally important for the church to respond to the needs of all families with planned educational programs so that the families are more able to meet the issues of daily life and resolve them before they *become* crises. Our commitment to empower families with practical tools for a richer life together and for Christian service is surely as basic and significant as our commitment to minister to families in crises.

By focusing on family ministry as our *educational* task, the role of the nonprofessional church leader is highlighted. After all, lay people have been in charge of church education programs for the past two hundred years! Just as lay leaders are trained to work with children and youth in the church, so lay leaders can learn the skills needed to work with families. When we see the educational dimension of family ministry, it ceases to be a mystery that only highly trained family counselors can begin to fathom. It becomes a task we can tackle. Planning teaching-learning events that will help parent and child, husband and wife, widow and grandniece to hear each other, enjoy each other, and discover God's Good News together is something you and I can feel comfortable doing.

2. Family Ministry Is a Theological Task

Family ministry takes place at the intersection of biblical insight and our best understanding of human development. It deals with daily life, with the give and take of human relationships, and with the utterly practical application of biblical truth to our daily experiences. Every family-ministry event must integrate three things: biblical teachings of God's will for our lives as members of a holy community, our daily experiences of family life, and what we know about how human relationships work. This kind of integration is a theological task. Family ministry in a teaching church always has this theological dimension. As church educators our concern is that the teachings of the Bible become concrete, practical, living guidelines as well as words of divine encouragement, helping us to bring forth the fruits of the Spirit in our most intimate relationships.

The questions and concerns we have about family life are some of the most sensitive we ever raise. They involve our sense of who we are as male and female persons; our self-esteem; and our deepest feelings about being a child, a parent, a spouse, and a sibling. Our most dearly held hopes for self, for our life partner, and for our offspring are the substance of family life.

These questions and concerns, cutting to the heart of our beings, are truly theological questions. The shape and character of our beliefs about God, sin, salvation, grace, and forgiveness are influenced mightily by the experiences we have as we grow up in a family and live in new partnerships as adults. Likewise, our beliefs influence the decisions we make about sexuality, marriage, parenthood, vocation, and life goals.

What this means is that family education can be done only in a theological context, in a community where what we value and how we interpret the meaning of human life are at the center of attention. The techniques of communication can indeed be learned anywhere, but the deeper meaning of human communication is a theological issue. Family education belongs in a teaching church where the theological power and significance of family experiences are recognized and honored.

In the Christian tradition there is a vision of the church as the family of God. This theological image of human relationship has much to offer us as persons and as family educators. It provides the freedom to take seriously as familial relationships those connections of person with person that seem to be outside the usual definitions of kinship. In the church family the friendship between a never-married woman of forty and a thirteen-year-old girl can be understood and celebrated! The newly married couple living a thousand miles from family and friends, the elderly couple who have no grandchildren of their own, the youth from a troubled home—all can find deep relationships within the church family to satisfy hungers for the intimacy and acceptance we all seek. Family ministry, as a theological task, evokes this vision of the church as God's family and puts it into practice.

3. Family Ministry Is an Advocacy Task

Family ministry grows out of a concern for the quality of life in family units. As Christian people we share a vision of the good life made possible when biblical mandates for justice, neighborliness, and respect for the worth of persons are honored and followed. This vision leads us to seek not only a high quality of personal relationships in family units but also a quality environment in which families can thrive.

In our biblical tradition, families are never seen in isolation but always as part of the wider community in society. Jesus' admonitions to take children seriously and the Old Testament mandate that parents shall nurture their children in the faith are not addressed only to nuclear family units. They are addressed to the whole community of faith in whose sheltering presence marriage covenants are established, parents bring up children, and widows and orphans are given special care. Therefore, from a biblical perspective the statistics about marriage and divorce, domestic violence, and teenage pregnancy or suicide lead us to raise questions about how the social environment impacts families. Clearly, the problems families experience are not simply expressions of "bad parents" or "rebellious youth" or "poor family dynamics." The problems that finally overwhelm families often come from outside the family unit.

The pressures on families are immense:

- Inflation raises havoc with family financial planning.
- Unemployment undermines parental self-esteem and authority, alienates youth from family and society, and condemns older persons to dependence.
- The high costs of energy and health care jeopardize the healthy development of children and force families to choose between heat and adequate medical care.
- The exploitation of sexuality in advertising and in the media undercuts the dignity of the human body and teaches false values to youth who are struggling to accept their own bodies and sexual feelings.
- Public resentment of subsidy programs for poor families, often exploited by ambitious politicians, prevents clear thinking about and intelligent public policy toward families left out of the economic mainstream.

Solutions to these kinds of problems require an informed public, intelligent and compassionate community leaders, and a vision of social justice. Christian congregations have an enormous contribution to make toward the solution of many of the problems facing families. Teaching churches are powerful public educators, contributing to an informed citizenry. Teaching churches nurture leaders for the community by helping persons discover their gifts for leadership, by providing a community of support, and by providing a vision of the good society. Biblical values of fairness toward persons with special needs, of honesty in the marketplace, of regard for individual conscience, of compassion for the poor, and of respect for the integrity of family relationships are crucial to public discussion of the pressures squeezing families. Christian people and congregations have a witness to make!

Christian congregations are also places where persons learn skills in running organizations, negotiating conflicts, and building consensus around common goals. These skills are needed by family members who must relate every day to school systems, governmental agencies, industrial bureaucracies, and all kinds of voluntary organizations from the scouts to the PTA. Family ministry includes helping youth and adults apply biblical values and insights to their relationships with these institutions. It includes teaching skills for working with and within the systems of which we are a part. And it includes supporting persons and groups as they seek to change these systems toward more just and more compassionate practices.

The tasks of family ministry, then, include being advocates for the needs of families with public authorities, teaching skills in community organization to youth and adults, and helping the whole congregation understand how economic and institutional systems both help and hurt families.

CHAPTER 2

The Content and Skill Areas of Family Ministry

Family ministry is concerned with three major content areas: growth in faith, sexuality, and family relationships. Programs of family education build concepts, provide information, and deepen understanding of self and others in these three areas.

CONTENT AREA #1: GROWTH IN FAITH

The life of faith is often pictured in the Bible as a journey or pilgrimage. As the pilgrim journeys, following God's leading, faith is deepened and life is enriched. The journey is growth producing. That Christian pilgrims should be about the task of growing in faith is expressed repeatedly in the New Testament. Jesus, a model of faith, "grew, both in body and in wisdom, gaining favor with God and men" (Luke 2:52, TEV). We are to "become mature [people], reaching to the very height of Christ's full stature" and "we must grow up in every way to Christ, who is the head" (Ephesians 4:13, 15, TEV). We are to grow from foundational teachings, which are like milk for babes, to the more meaty wisdom of mature, adult faith (Hebrews 5:12-14). While all of us once spoke, felt, and thought as children, we are challenged to give up childish ways when we become adults (1 Corinthians 13:11). The concept of growth in faith is a basic one and has many implications for family ministries. Not surprisingly, then, contemporary theologians and Christian educators are paying more attention to the process and pattern of growth in faith. Books on the steps of faith development are becoming more common, and some are inspiring Christian educators to think in new ways about how we can best encourage growth in faith.

Human beings do in fact grow in their understanding of their relationship with God and in their ability to respond to God with

trust and love. Growth in faith does not end with childhood or
adolescence but continues throughout the adult years. The faith
issues that are most significant to us tend to shift as we mature.

Faith, of course, involves the whole of one's personhood, the
unconscious and unspoken aspects of personality as well as the
conscious and overt aspects. The youngest baby is involved in faith
development as she begins to develop a sense of basic trust in
relationship to persons in her environment. Younger children
whose initiative sometimes results in accidents or punishment for
infractions against the laws of nature or society, struggle with what
it means to make mistakes or commit wrongs, seek forgiveness,
and then experience reconciliation. Adolescents' search for belong-
ing and for a sense of personal identity is reflected through their
desire to belong to the Christian community while at the same
time needing to search and test their inherited faith tradition by
questioning and probing.

When we understand faith development, we will not expect an
adolescent to be able to make the kind of faith commitment an
adult can make after a period of searching and testing. Owned
faith, faith that is strong enough to build a life upon, is the hard-
won prize of adulthood; still, faith continues to grow throughout
the adult years. The challenges, stresses, and achievements of one's
adult pilgrimage demand theological reflection. Facing the inevi-
table tragedies and receiving grace in the midst of trial give shape
to one's spiritual growth.

Family education that focuses on faith development helps the
whole congregation understand how persons of different ages and
at different points in the life cycle are also at different points in their
understanding and practice of faith. Challenging persons to grow,
supporting them in the struggle toward an owned faith, and being
partners in the journey are among the ways the teaching congregation can enrich the faith development of persons.

Growth in faith is not an automatic consequence of growing
older. That persons will respond to God's Spirit moving in their
lives cannot be guaranteed, but family educators can prepare the
way for faith development by paying attention to several important
dimensions of human growth.

A. The first dimension of growth involves physical and mental
development—the changes in patterns of thinking and acting that
take place as persons mature. Teachers of children are aware of the
ways of thinking that are characteristic of children at different
chronological ages. We know that children's ability to think and
act grows as they age chronologically and as their nervous systems

mature. Concepts which are literally unthinkable by a four-year-old can be handled with ease by a ten-year-old. Physical activities which are impossible for the six-year-old are routine for the twelve-year-old. While such developmental changes in children and adolescents are widely recognized, we are only beginning to understand that developmental processes of growth take place in adults as well. We are beginning to understand that adults characteristically learn in ways which are different from the ways children and youth learn. Understanding these patterns of physical and mental development helps us to approach other aspects of how humans develop.

B. Just as human beings develop physically and mentally, they also develop emotionally and socially. We grow in our capacity to form relationships and in our capacity to feel and comprehend a wider and more differentiated range of emotions. Each stage of human development involves important tasks in building emotional bonds:

- The infant learns to distinguish between self and another.
- The young child learns to relate to siblings and peers.
- The adolescent seeks to define self as a separate entity from the family and as a member of a peer group.
- The young adult works at learning how to establish intimacy in a relationship.
- Young people seek mentors who will guide their development as workers and participants in the wider community.
- Middle adults become mentors, work at being parents, and have the task of growing in intimacy through marriage or some other close relationship.
- Older adults face the task of closing relationships as their peers die, as their careers come to an end, and as their own deaths approach.

Every stage of human life involves tasks of emotional development which can be profoundly significant to every person.

C. Development also takes place in the moral realm. Recent research has helped to clarify the patterns of growth in the capacity of persons to identify and own their values and to reason through moral dilemmas. We are now aware that the patterns of moral reasoning used by children change as the children mature and that the appropriate educational experiences can enable adults, as well as children, to grow in the breadth and depth of their moral thinking. Research on moral development has uncovered two facts of great significance for family education:

- First, children and youth grow in their ability to think through moral dilemmas when they are exposed to the more sophisticated moral thinking of older persons. Thus, intergenerational relationships are crucial for growth in moral thinking.

● Second, most people are stuck at less mature levels of moral reasoning because they have not been challenged to exercise their capacity to reason through moral dilemmas.

It is precisely in the community of faith where such challenge, struggle, and growth are most possible. A central focus of family education needs to be helping persons grow toward the kind of moral maturity and vision we see portrayed in the living and teaching of Jesus Christ.

Knowledge of how humans develop physically, mentally, emotionally, socially, and morally contributes to mature self-understanding. Such knowledge and understanding help parents appreciate the behavior, feelings, and decisions of their children.

Programs of family education do two important things. First, they build knowledge and understanding of human growth and development; second, they provide experiences which challenge children, youth, and adults to take the next step in development. When these various developmental tasks are interpreted in the light of the life and teachings of Jesus, the way is prepared for a step in faith development as well. By focusing on concepts of human development, family ministry not only helps persons and families move through times of growth, but also opens the way for them to respond to their growing pains in faith.

CONTENT AREA #2: SEXUALITY

A second content area in family education is sexuality. We know that the family is the primary context in which persons develop both consciously and unconsciously as sexual beings. In the family, sex-role attitudes and behaviors are modeled by parents and learned by children. Fundamental attitudes toward one's body and toward the bodies of others are unconsciously learned at home. One's basic appreciation of maleness and femaleness is profoundly influenced by the attitude and practices of one's family. Generally, in our culture, families require support and help for their home to become a place where children understand, accept, and value their sexuality.

We are living through a time of marked changes in attitudes toward sexuality and the expression of sexual feelings. Men and women within and outside of the Christian community are changing their self-understanding of what it means to be a male or female person. The traditional linkage of sexual expression, marriage, and childbearing has broken down. Decisions to be sexually active, to be married, or to parent a child are now experienced as quite separate decisions.

Some of this change is due to the new contraceptives. Some of it is due to a growing understanding of sexual expression as an adult human right. Persons heretofore excluded from consideration as sexual beings, for example, the elderly and persons with disabilities, are now seen to be fully human (and, therefore, sexual) with the right to express their sexuality.

Statistics indicate that the majority of American youth have experienced sexual intercourse by the age of seventeen. The percentage of households made up of unmarried, cohabiting couples has increased dramatically in the last fifteen years. The visibility of persons with a homosexual orientation has increased. Church people and organizations are being challenged to reexamine their attitudes toward nonmarital sexual expression.

These changes cannot be ignored. Coupled with the media's exploitation of sexuality both in programming and in advertising, they cause families to feel an increasing responsibility to be the sex educators of children and youth. Parents are being challenged to think about the kinds of sexual experiences they want for their children and the kinds of sexual experiences they hope their children will avoid. The church is virtually the only organization to which whole families belong and, therefore, has both enormous responsibility and opportunity to help families deal with their feelings and values in the area of sexuality.

Helping families to obtain accurate information about sexuality is important. Of even greater importance is helping families establish a climate where the divinely created goodness of sexuality is reverenced, appreciated, and affirmed. Because a teaching church is committed to nurturing persons in Christian growth, it will continue to be concerned for the development in persons of a healthy sexuality linked to a genuine regard for self and others.

CONTENT AREA #3: FAMILY RELATIONSHIPS

How family members relate to one another within the household and to the world beyond their family unit constitutes a third content area for family ministry. This content area has to do with a family's integration of faith commitments, values, needs, and goals into a pattern of life with a Christian character. Concerns here include:

- Bringing to bear biblical insights about human relationships and moral choices on family experience;
- Understanding how relationships within the family between the spouses, among siblings, and between generations change over the family life cycle;
- Enriching the relationship between the family unit and the congregation;

- Understanding the relationships of family units to the larger community, especially to the schooling, economic, political, and social welfare systems.

A key concept is the "family system." This means seeing a family as a whole, as a system that is more than simply the sum of its parts. With this understanding, it is easy to see that changes experienced by one family member affect all the others. Family systems operate by rules, usually unstated ones, and include unconscious agreements about the role each family member will play. Changes in these patterns of rules and roles impact every member of a family system and determine to a significant degree how well that individual person functions at home and elsewhere.

Consider what happens when a mother who has been working as a full-time homemaker moves into employment outside the home. Her role changes. New demands and expectations from her employer require her to make significant changes in the way she relates to her family. Tension and pain for her and other family members are likely unless the *system* changes and the other family members shift their roles. New agreements about roles, new rules for getting the family's work done, and new patterns of communicating and decision making have to be negotiated.

Learning to see our family units as systems helps us to appreciate more fully the contribution each member makes to the whole. Understanding the concept of the "family system" helps families choose and grow into patterns of living together that liberate, fulfill, and satisfy each member.

Understanding how a family unit relates to the larger community is another important aspect of this content area. The Christian family is a potential unit of mission. The daily routines of taking out the garbage, gardening, buying gasoline, recycling the newspapers, and preparing meals can make each family member deeply aware of the needs of the global village. The familial household is a potential laboratory where nonviolent methods of solving conflicts can be experienced and learned. Home is the place where our most personal learnings about justice occur and where a vision of how to live in God's presence takes form. The choices church-related families make about how to spend their income and apply their skills as leaders or participants in the social and political life of the wider community are major avenues of witness. Family units who work at managing their finances in a responsible way or undertake projects to help disadvantaged and oppressed persons not only strengthen their life as a family but also communicate the Good News of Jesus Christ more powerfully than a hundred sermons. Families need not be simply victims of social changes; they can be and often are the initiators of social change. Family ministry in a teaching church has as one of its tasks preparing, inspiring, and assisting families to fulfill this part of their Christian vocation.

In addition to these three content areas of central concern to family life education (growth in faith, sexuality, and family relationships), three skill areas are of major significance.

SKILL AREA #1: COMMUNICATION SKILLS

Fulfilling family relationships obviously depend upon the ability of family members to communicate clearly with one another. Marriages flounder when communication is inadequate. Parents and children become enemies for the same reason. Probably no aspect of family life education is so important and so practical. Communication skill training includes learning how to:

- Speak for one's self;
- Disclose self-awareness of sensations, feelings, thoughts, intentions, and behavior;
- Listen effectively to another;
- Clarify what another is saying and meaning;
- Negotiate solutions to conflicts;
- Build self-esteem and respect for others.

Training in communication skills is education for the prevention of crises which require counseling. Communication skills are needed by every family, and the reward for improvement in communication is immediate, long-lasting, and immensely satisfying to family members.

SKILL AREA #2: PLANNING SKILLS

Well-functioning families plan their life together. Families are continually confronted with situations and opportunities which require planning. Some common examples are:

- Planning family spending,
- Planning for the care of aging family members,
- Planning leisure activities,
- Planning for education and careers.

Christian families are characterized by intentional living. This means a pattern of life together that reflects the values of the gospel. Intentional living requires planning skills. The ability to plan together enriches family interaction and leads to greater family unity and satisfaction in family relationships.

SKILL AREA #3: ORGANIZATIONAL SKILLS

Family ministry is concerned with empowering families. The complexity of organizations, economic forces, and the pluralism of values in one's community can leave families feeling overwhelmed and overpowered. In our culture, family units relate to all manner of social institutions: schools, PTAs, Little Leagues, town councils, the courts, welfare departments, employers, unions, and government. Generally, the institutions of our society are not designed to respond effectively to family units. Some of these institutions, in fact, seem to operate in ways that put stress on families. So it is not enough to understand how organizations in the society affect one's family; one also needs *skill in negotiating with bureaucracies* and *skill in building coalitions with other families* to encourage and sometimes compel major institutions to respect the integrity of families.

Parents, older children, and youth need skill training to help them

- relate positively to the many persons who represent important institutions, e.g., teachers, guidance counselors, police, employers, union leaders;
- cooperate with other families to identify and shape the policies of the major institutions so that family life is helped or at least respected;
- negotiate in complex situations with, for example, the administrators of schools, the leaders of businesses, the employees of government agencies;
- initiate coalitions with other families or groups when neighborhood, community, or other issues arise which seriously affect family life.

Families do not exist in isolation but rather at the focal point of some of the most powerful social forces moving our culture. In order to maintain Christian patterns of family living, it is essential that Christian families have organizing skills. Christian families possessing such skills can make a difference for their neighbors and community and in the large institutions that shape their lives.

CHAPTER 3

The Biblical Foundation of Family Ministry

A commitment to nurturing persons in Christian growth leads to a concern for the quality of life within families. The faith development of children and youth is most profoundly influenced by their parents. The vitality of a marriage reflects the Christian maturity of the partners and contributes to their further growth as Christian believers. One's acceptance of self as a sexual being and as a responsible spirit is formed chiefly in the home. Spiritually, much hangs on the quality of the home.

Central to a ministry of the church is, of course, the biblical foundation for that ministry. Let us consider several important texts that underlie and shape our concepts of family ministry.

FAMILIES NURTURE FAITH IN CHILDREN

Deuteronomy 6:4-9 is the classic text for family ministry, a text that places on the home primary responsibility for nurturing faith in children:

> "Israel, remember this! The LORD—and the LORD alone—is our God. Love the LORD your God with all your heart, with all your soul, and with all your strength. Never forget these commands that I am giving you today. Teach them to your children. Repeat them when you are at home and when you are away, when you are resting and when you are working. Tie them on your arms and wear them on your foreheads as a reminder. Write them on the doorposts of your houses and on your gates" (TEV).

The picture of faith nurture which these verses paint is not that of a "school" at all. The picture is not one of time set aside for classes in religious instruction; rather it is one of an integrated everyday life which is colored with conversations and symbols to remind each family member of the Great Commandment. The decorations in the house, the ornaments worn by individual family members, and the family talk—all carry reminders of God's presence. Whatever one is doing at any moment in a family's life is done before God. Nurture in the faith is continual and continuous with the ordinary activities of everyday life. The faith is passed on, not through prepared speeches, but through the ordinary activities of life, which have all been marked in some way by reverence for God and remembrance of God's teachings.

What we discover from behavioral science about how families influence the learning and development of children is completely consistent with this biblical picture of how religious nurture takes place. For example, in homes where adults read, where there are magazines and books, children generally learn to read early and begin formal schooling with basic reading skills already in place. Increasingly, professional educators are coming to believe that families are the *primary educators* of children and that what happens at home conditions what can happen for a child in a school. Again, the picture is not of parents who sit down and deliberately teach children to read, but of parents for whom reading is simply a part of everyday life.

At the same time, unaided family units will probably not be able to fulfill their responsibilities to nurture the next generation "in the fear and admonition of the Lord." Interestingly, the Bible almost never uses the word "family" to refer to what we call a nuclear family. Family nearly always means the clan, the tribe, the extended group who stand with and around each couple and each parent-child unit. Contemporary family units need the supportive presence of the extended family of God, the local congregation, in order to nurture their members in Christian growth.

Jesus accented the responsibility of the whole community for children in several sayings about children:

> Some people brought children to Jesus for him to place his hands on them, but the disciples scolded the people. When Jesus noticed this, he was angry and said to his disciples, "Let the children come to me, and do not stop them, because the Kingdom of God belongs to such as these. I assure you that whoever does not receive the Kingdom of God like a little child will never enter it" (Mark 10:13-15, TEV).

> So Jesus called a child, had him stand in front of them, and said, "I assure you that unless you change and become like children, you will never enter the Kingdom of heaven. The greatest in the Kingdom of heaven is the one who humbles himself and becomes like this child.

And whoever welcomes in my name one such child as this, welcomes me" (Matthew 18:2-6, TEV).

Consistent with Jesus' pattern of exalting those of low degree, he places children at the very center of his ministry and challenges those adults who would follow him to take the child as a model of faith. Indeed, the response of a disciple to the needs of a child is nothing less than a response to Jesus himself. For Jesus a key test of the quality of a Christian community's life is the way it treats the children in its midst.

JESUS AFFIRMED AND LIMITED "FAMILY"

Jesus' attitudes toward family realities are complex. For instance, in Luke 2:41-51 we find the picture of Jesus as a young adolescent. In keeping with the developmental task of that period, Jesus is putting some distance between himself and his family. We see him in the temple striking out in some new directions; rather than simply following Joseph into carpentry, he engages the teachers in questions and answers. In these verses we see Jesus forging an identity that is not simply the product of his family of origin, one that is certainly not the fulfillment of his parents' expectations. His parents are understandably distressed and baffled by his behavior. Yet, at the same time, Jesus consciously submits himself to his parents' discipline. There is both resistance to family expectations and acceptance of family obligations and nurture.

As an adult and as a preacher and prophet, Jesus' relationship with his family was not smooth. His family was not supportive of his ministry. In the seventh chapter of John, Jesus' brothers offer him much advice, and the Gospel writer comments, "Even his brothers did not believe in him." The most dramatic confrontation between Jesus and his family is described in the third chapter of Mark. Jesus has returned home; the crowds are enormous; and his family is ready to believe the judgments of the religious authorities that Jesus is either mad or possessed by the devil. When his family comes to take him home, Jesus refuses to see them. In verses 33-35 Jesus redefines the family in a radical way: "Who are my mother and my brothers? . . . Here are my mother and brothers! Whoever does the will of God is my brother, and sister, and mother." Jesus' kin are those who share a commitment to the kingdom. A more radical challenge to the ordinary understanding of the family has never been given! Let all who (sometimes self-righteously) define "Christian family" in narrow terms take note!

At the same time that Jesus proclaimed and lived a loyalty to the kingdom which transcends family ties, Jesus did not forget his obligations as a firstborn son. In Mark 7:9-13 Jesus rebukes the Pharisees who found in their religious traditions a way to avoid their obligations to care for aging parents. Jesus acted out his own responsibility toward his mother when, on the cross, he entrusted her to the care of his beloved disciple (John 19:26-27).

There is in the Gospels an astounding honesty about Jesus' family. His brothers and mother were prominent members of the first Christian group in Jerusalem, yet the stories of the tensions between Jesus and his family were preserved in oral tradition and finally in the written Gospels. Jesus underscores the positive potential of family life and at the same time challenges the church to be a familial fellowship which transcends the limitations of any and every particular family group.

A BIBLICAL APPROACH TO FAMILY MINISTRY

Our motivation for family ministry is in response to the biblical insight that families are the key to nurturing faith in children and youth. Our approach to family ministry is governed by Jesus' teaching and example. From him we learn to appreciate both the positive potential and the valid limitations of family life.

- Just as Jesus enjoyed the warmth of family gatherings in the homes of Peter and of Mary and Martha and celebrated marriage as a symbol of the kingdom, so family ministry supports, affirms, and celebrates the strength of family life.

- Just as Jesus had compassion for parents of sick children and recognized that parents know how to give good things to their children in spite of sin and limitation, so family ministry seeks to support parents in nurturing the faith development of their children.

- Just as Jesus recognized the inevitability of conflict in family groups when the ultimate claims of discipleship are faced, so family ministry recognizes the need for Christian congregations to be the more inclusive family in which the brokenness and limitations of particular families are transcended and sometimes healed.

Family ministry will help parents understand the need of adolescent children to test parental values and wisdom. Family ministry will help adolescents understand the motivation and developmental needs of parents. A family ministry that is faithful to the ministry of Jesus will never exclude persons whose family life has been disrupted by divorce or whose family system includes more than those who are related by blood, marriage, or adoption. Family ministry that is faithful to the ministry of Jesus will recognize as

Christian families those partial family units who share in the life of the congregation even though a spouse or a child or a parent does not participate.

BLENDING HIGH EXPECTATION WITH COMPASSION

Jesus had great expectations for marriage and family life. He saw marriage as a covenant between two persons to "do life together for life," and he assumed as a matter of course that parents would seek the welfare of their children. Yet Jesus had great compassion for those who missed the mark, even those who were at fault, as is revealed by his conversation with the woman at the well and his dramatic response to the woman accused of adultery.

The apostle Paul reflects the spirit of Jesus as he applies Jesus' teaching to the particular circumstances of particular families in the church at Corinth. In the seventh chapter of First Corinthians Paul deals with the question of marriage and divorce as it arises in a variety of circumstances not explicitly addressed in Jesus' teaching. For example, with genuine pastoral sensitivity Paul counsels believers to remain wedded to unbelieving spouses for the sake of the children and, ultimately, for the sake of the spouse. At the same time he recognizes that such marriages may indeed end and counsels the believing spouse to be at peace with that possibility and reality.

Paul's pastoral application of Christian teaching to particular circumstances of family life provides a model for our efforts in family ministry. Our challenge is to apply our best insights from the biblical tradition to the realities of family living today and to do so with a full measure of compassion and the willingness to grapple with circumstances not foreseen by biblical writers.

THE CHRISTIAN HOUSEHOLD

The most elaborate discussion of a familial household in the New Testament is found in Ephesians, chapters 5 and 6. The passage discusses the duties and responsibilities of the husband-father-master, the wife-mother, the children, and the servants. This list of duties is not unlike the lists from Stoic literature contemporary with the book of Ephesians, which outlined household responsibilities in a similar way. The striking difference between the biblical list and the Stoic lists is that the biblical writer addressed all members of the household as responsible persons who have choices and rights. In the Stoic lists, everyone in the household is simply the property of the male head of the house and responsible to him. Obviously the biblical writer had a much different view of the personhood of women, children, and servants.

The other important observation to make about this passage is that the key verse is Ephesians 5:21. It is addressed to the husband and wife: "Be subject to one another out of reverence for Christ." Clearly there is no pitting of husband against wife or placing husband over wife. Rather we find a confession of faith that in a Christian family Christ is the head of the household and all members of the household are mutually responsible to one another and to Christ. Mutual submission to Christ provides the framework within which the duties and responsibilities of each household member are spelled out.

The Bible mandates ministry focused on families. In the biblical view the family is a key to faith development for its members. Our ministry to families is always shaped by biblical insight. The congregation of believers is called to be a familial group that both reinforces the strengths of smaller family units and overcomes the failures of individual family systems. The power of family ministry to make a difference in people's lives arises from a Christlike acceptance of all persons.

In the next chapter we will examine today's changing families to whom family ministry is directed.

CHAPTER 4

Changing Families and Family Ministry

Much is being written and said about families today in the press, on television, and in books. The shortcomings of family life in America have been well-documented and widely publicized. Some accuse the family of oppressing women, stifling individual emotional health, and creating a violence-prone society. Others predict the demise of the family as it is currently understood and its replacement by communal child rearing and living-together arrangements unsanctioned by license or clergy. Church leaders may be tempted to think of family ministry as a crisis ministry in response to the "death" of the family.

Indeed, exploiting the uneasiness church people feel about changes in family life is becoming a common tactic of some political pressure groups. Proposals for day-care programs or infant and child-feeding programs are criticized as "attacks on the traditional family." Self-styled "profamily" leaders lobby against efforts to secure equal rights for women, disparage attempts to provide sex education and counseling to youth, urge upon us the restoration of daily school prayers, and advocate massive shifts of public monies from social programs to military weapons all in the name of the "family."

Caught in the middle of such contradictory claims and emotions, church leaders may have difficulty knowing just what *is* happening to families in the 1980s.

SOME IMPORTANT CHANGES

There *are* significant changes taking place in the patterns of marriage and divorce, in the expression of sexuality, and in the roles of family members. It is natural to wonder what is happening to the family when over the last decade:

- the divorce rate continued to rise;
- the number of unmarried couples living together tripled;
- the two-income household became the most typical family pattern;
- domestic violence was found to be a feature of life for many families;
- the proportion of children living in single-parent homes approached 20 percent.

These changes and others have been taking place among church-related families as well as the unchurched. Consequently, pastors and other church leaders are confronted with the need to develop new ministries and deepen traditional ones. Loud critics and loud defenders of the so-called "traditional" family are heard within and without the church. Family life has become a controversial issue!

THE ROOTS OF CHANGE

The controversy swirling around family life today has its roots in the social changes of the 1960s and the reaction to those changes. In the 1960s many groups in American life saw themselves living under restriction, excluded from full participation in society, and denied recognition and power. These groups began to challenge the conditions and customs they identified as responsible for their situation. These liberation movements had an effect on families and on thinking about families.

For example, the black liberation movement challenged prevailing white academic opinion that black families were dysfunctional. Researchers and writers began to identify the strengths of black family life, especially the remarkable capacity of black neighborhood and community groups to function as extended families for their members. A new appreciation emerged for the terrible burdens of history and the present social circumstances borne by black families.

But it was probably the rising consciousness of women and their challenge to the customs, laws, and practices based on the subordination of women that has contributed the most to the sense that the family is somehow changing. Actually, the growing insistence of women on full participation in society is a worldwide phenomenon with roots that extend back well over a hundred years. Many women in the church, and men, too, participate in and welcome the changing role of women. Some Christians resist these changes in the conviction that there is a "true" or biblical family form, which God has ordained and in which the male-husband-father is head, superior, and ruler.

Such a male supremacist understanding of family life is simply not biblical, as we have seen. There is not one word from the lips of Jesus that says to women: "Keep your place." Indeed, in his conversation with Mary and Martha, Jesus makes just the opposite point! It is also worth noting that the household of Martha and Mary hardly fits the picture of the "traditional" family that some would hold up as the God-appointed ideal.

This is a good time for Christians to remember that patterns of family living have, in fact, shifted several times over the course of Christian history. If we look at the development of family life in Christianized societies since the New Testament days, we will search in vain for a normative Christian form. In rural areas of continental Europe, even up until the nineteenth century, an extended three-generation, patriarchal family was the rule. Marriages were arranged by parents more with an eye to inheritance and the accumulation of family farmlands than to the needs or desires of the couple. In contrast, in England as far back as records go, the two-generation family unit of parents and children has been the norm. Both patterns of family life came to this country with the European immigrants.

Clearly, preoccupation with the form of families is unhelpful. A more helpful concern, one with a clear biblical foundation, is the quality of relationships within familial households. Planners of family ministry need to ask themselves: What are the facts about family relationships today and what are the needs and opportunities for ministry?

THE FACTS OF CHANGE

Certainly, part of the concern about families today is because of the divorce rate. During the period from 1966 to 1976, the divorce rate doubled. Since 1976, however, the rate has leveled off. The marriage rate, which declined during the 1973-1975 period, stabilized in the mid-seventies and has increased steadily since 1977. Some of the gloomier prophecies about the future of family life were based on the upsurge in the divorce rate and decline in the marriage rate. These trends from the sixties and seventies have not persisted and may have been caused by changes in the makeup of our population. The huge baby boom of the postwar period led to an enormous expansion in the number of young adults during the 1960s. This increase in the number of young adults led to a dramatic increase in the number of marriages followed by a dramatic increase in the number of divorces; this in turn was followed by the leveling off of the marriage rate. As the baby-boom generation ages, we now see a stabilizing of the divorce rate and a pickup in the marriage rate, which includes remarriages.

With the increase in divorce has come an increase in single-parent homes. Nearly 20 percent of children experience a single-parent home before the age of eighteen, a threefold increase since 1970. A smaller but significant number also experience a "reconstituted" or "blended" family when divorced parents remarry. Such households often include children from one or both previous marriages and possibly children born to the new union. The stresses on children moving through separation, divorce, and remarriage are severe.

Another change that has contributed to concern about family life is the dramatic increase in the number of unmarried-couple households. Unmarried-couple households account for only 2 percent of all households, although that is triple the number of just ten years ago. Twenty-seven percent of such households include children.

Teenage sexual activity has increased, and the rate of teenage pregnancy has become a major social concern. Venereal disease is epidemic among the teenage population. Unwed motherhood is increasingly common and occurs among all socioeconomic groups.

Finally, there has been over the last decade a massive movement of women into the paid labor force. The most typical two-parent household is now one in which the mother is employed at least part-time outside of the home. This change has not yet been followed by significant changes in homemaking roles. that is, the wives and mothers employed outside the home still do more of the childcare and housecare than do husbands and fathers.

THE PERSISTENCE OF FAMILIES

Yet in spite of all the changes over the past twenty years, families remain a central fact of American life. It is important to note that most persons marry and most marriages last until the death of a partner (which means, on the average, fifty years!) Two-thirds of all households are made up of "traditional families" of a married couple with or without children. While the number of children desired is typically fewer, the percentage of couples planning on children is as high as ever. In poll after poll, Americans affirm that a good family life is one of their most sought-after values.

Sociologists observing households today would see:

- Married couples with children;
- A single parent with children;
- Two mothers and their children;

- Married couples without children or with grown children;
- Father, mother, and children from previous marriages;
- Unmarried couples;
- Single persons;
- Married and unmarried adults plus children sharing space, income, housework, and, in some cases, religious or political values;
- Two adults of the same sex living together permanently;
- Religious orders and communities.

In addition, an observer today will find here and there groups of two-generation family units, couples, and single persons who have formed themselves into self-declared extended families. They may share an apartment house or a neighborhood and seek deliberately to fulfill the function of kin to one another. An observer also will note that the extended family is alive and well. The typical American has contact with an extended family member once a week. And telephone company records would suggest that those who do not see one another are nevertheless very much in touch with one another.

Underneath these changes in the working patterns of women, in the divorce rate, in the number of unmarried couples, and in the number of single-parent households, there are deep and stable currents of family life which shape the experiences of most of us. Often family ministry is seen mainly as a response to the crises experienced by persons undergoing a divorce or facing an unwed pregnancy or making a decision whether to marry or simply live together. However, it is also important to see family ministry as a response to the stable currents of family life. The focus of family ministry should be on long-term relationships, those which have a history and an expected future. Not surprisingly, people continue to want and need these kinds of relationships. Family ministry is concerned with enriching them.

THE AUDIENCES FOR FAMILY MINISTRY

For our purposes, then, it may be useful to define "family" as "two or more persons related by blood, marriage, adoption, covenant, or mutual consent." Our emphasis is not on family structures but on the quality of the relationships within family structures and the potential of those relationships for fostering individual growth.

Who then are the audiences for family ministry?

- First and foremost are *married couples*. This is the key family relationship on which much else depends. The basic health of the family system is a function of the marriage relationship.

Family ministry needs to focus on the married couple as the fundamental relationship.

- Because the marriage relationship is so vital, ministry with *persons whose marriages have died* is essential. Whether death or divorce has ended the relationship, persons who have lost a marital partner are experiencing the greatest stress known and both counseling and educational ministries are needed.
- *Parents and their children* also need to be the focus of family ministry. Parenthood is one of the few occupations for which no training is provided! Helping parents to function effectively and in satisfying ways with their children is a basic educational task of the church. Providing parents with opportunities for learning communications skills and understanding the patterns of child development is key. It is equally important to nurture the capacity of parents for theological reflection since they will make the most significant contribution to the religious understanding of their children. Parents are almost always a child's most powerful teachers.
- A special area of ministry with parents is ministry with *single parents*. Raising children without a marital partner is some of the hardest work there is! Single parents even more than "double parents" need the safety net of a support network.
- Other audiences for family life education include *grandparents, youth, and single people,* who often have concerns about relating more effectively to their own families of origin and are often interested in relating to the children and youth of other households.

The biblical image of the church as the family of God inspires a vision of the local congregation as an extended family. There is a sense, then, in which the whole congregation is an audience for family ministry. Building a climate that encourages persons to reach out to one another as kin is a major hoped-for outcome of family ministry.

Because every congregation is unique, defining the audiences for family ministry is a different task in every congregation. The following chapter describes how a congregation can define the audiences for family ministry and how that ministry can be planned.

CHAPTER 5

Steps to Planning Family Ministries

This chapter is written for several kinds of planning groups:
- A local church board, committee of Christian education, or task force on family ministry;
- A family-ministry team representing several congregations in a denominational association, area, or conference;
- An ecumenical family-ministry team drawn from the churches in a town or county;
- A committee jointly appointed by churches and community groups to plan programs for strengthening families.

In order to provide family-ministry programs that will be helpful to specific kinds of families, most congregations will need to work cooperatively with others in their denomination or community. The planning process offered here is based on this assumption.

It is vital that a family-ministry planning team be formed that includes both men and women. The experiences and meanings of marriage, parenthood, and sexuality are markedly different for the two sexes. Male and female perspectives on the family need to be present when family-ministry programs are being planned. It is also helpful if a range of ages is represented on the team. The issues of family life are different for different age groups.

At minimum, then, a family-ministry planning team needs to include a man and a woman. A maximum size for a workable planning group is probably about seven persons.

Use this chapter:
- As a framework for beginning family ministry in your church,
- As an agenda for the planning group,
- As a guide to annual planning for family ministry,
- As a resource for uncovering areas where you need to supplement and strengthen what you are already doing in family ministry.

The planning process presented here has six steps: identifying needs, writing objectives, discovering resources, developing program plans, testing these plans, and evaluating the program.

1. IDENTIFY NEEDS

There are three parts to this step:
- *First,* determine who the families in your church are.
- *Second,* find out what their needs are.
- *Third,* determine to which needs you will give priority.

Who Are the Families in Your Church?

To help you begin to answer this question, look at the "Family Life Cycle Chart" (on page 39) which depicts the cycle through which a family moves from formation to dissolution. The chart is a way of looking at an intergenerational family system which changes over time. You may want to photocopy the chart or reproduce it on newsprint so all members of the planning group can see it. As a family system evolves, its needs change. Part of who the families in your church are is a question of *where* the family systems are in their life cycles.

To help you focus on *where your church families are in their life cycles,* put each one of these headings on a separate sheet of newsprint (or write the heading across the top of a chalkboard):

Recently married couples
Families with preschool children
Families with school-age children
Families with teenage children
Families with children leaving/gone from home
Retired persons or couples
Widowed persons

Under each heading list the families in your church who are at that point in the family life cycle. Some families may be listed under more than one heading.

To identify *the kinds of family households in your congregation,* write each of the following headings on a separate sheet of newsprint or across the chalkboard:

Married couple
Two parents with a single income
Two parents with a dual income
Single parent

FAMILY LIFE CYCLE CHART

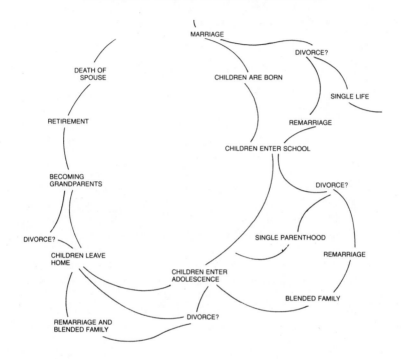

Remarried couple
Remarried couple with children from a previous and or present
  union
Three generations

In your church family there will be other kinds of households you
may want to recognize, for example single-person households or
brother-sister households. Under each heading, list the names of
persons or families who fall into that household category. Again,
some names may appear on more than one list. By listing your
church families according to their stage in the family life cycle and
according to their type of household, you have begun to identify
the different kinds of family systems present in your church. You
have answered the question "Who are the families in your church?"

What Are the Needs of Families in Your Church?

Four methods to determine the needs of families in your church are suggested here. Use the method that seems most appropriate to your congregation and to the preferences of your planning group. You may choose to use two methods in combination. Each has its special strengths.

The first method is to brainstorm a list of possible needs. Choose one kind of familial household, for example, a single-parent household. Write the name of that kind of household at the top of the sheet of newsprint. Then brainstorm a list of all the needs this familial household might have. Be specific and concrete. Try to enter into the experience of this household imaginatively and ask yourself what life must be like for this kind of family? Look again at the "Family Life Cycle Chart." How will the needs of this kind of family change as it moves through the family life cycle? After you have listed the needs which a particular type of familial household has, circle those needs which you believe can be met by family-ministry programs. Repeat this process for all of the households that you have identified in your congregation.

A second method for determining family needs is to interview families. Invite representative families to meet with your planning group. Choose families from as many different kinds of households as you have in your congregation. Invite entire family units, including children, youth, and adults, to spend a one-to-two-hour session sharing what living in their kind of family system is like. Ask each family to list on newsprint what they see as their *needs* and their special *strengths*. After sharing needs and strengths, invite each family unit to take its turn before the group completing a sentence such as:
- The church could help our family by . . . .
- Our family would feel affirmed in its strengths if . . . .
- We wish the church would . . . .

The insights and suggestions generated by this kind of exchange should provide an ample agenda for family-ministry planners! You might consider meeting with these families again to set priorities. If you choose not to involve them this heavily, you will at least want to test your list of priority needs with these or other representative family units in your congregation.

A third method for identifying the needs of families in your congregation is to conduct a survey. There are several approaches you can take:
- Interview a number of family units at home. To do this you will want to call on the family at a time when all the members of the household can be present. You will find some suggested interview questions on page 42.

- Conduct a telephone survey in which you interview a representative sample of church members over the telephone.
- Use a checklist. A suggested checklist is on page 43.

A fourth way to collect information about the needs of families is to interview experts such as family therapists, school guidance counselors, social workers, your pastor, or a professor of family studies at a local college. You can also read about the needs of families. Several helpful books are listed in the Bibliography. A highly recommended resource for identifying the needs of families is the book *How's Your Family?* by Jerry M. Lewis, M.D. This book is based on research into the question "What makes a healthy family?" The research was done with church-related, middle-class families in the southwestern part of the United States. The book includes questionnaires useful in gathering information from families about their needs.

What Family Needs Are Priorities for Family Ministry?

As you look at the different family systems and their needs, you will see that a number of needs are common to the households you have identified. Families who are at the same stage in their family life cycles will have needs in common. For example, you may discover that married couples at several points along the life cycle have a need for training in communication skills or for times of enrichment and spiritual refreshment in their marriages. You will also feel that several of the needs you have identified are more pressing than others. Such reflections lead to setting priorities. Obviously, it is not possible to respond to everything all at once so you will have to choose one or two needs on which to focus. You might choose those that seem the most pressing or the most widespread. You might decide that enriching marriages should be your first priority since the marriage relationship is central to family structure and the key to family health. On the other hand, you may be a congregation which has many single parents, and you may wish to reach out to these families. Or again, the families with teenagers in your congregation may be feeling the most pressure and needing immediate attention. Every congregation will have its own sense of priorities.

Once you have begun to determine priorities, you would be wise to check them out with representative families in the congregation.

2. WRITE OBJECTIVES

After you have identified the needs of families in your congre-
(continued on page 44)

FAMILY MINISTRY INTERVIEW GUIDE

USE QUESTIONS FROM THIS GUIDE:

- to gather information on the telephone from families about their needs;
- to talk in a meeting with a group of several representative families from your congregation;
- to gather information about family needs when you call on families in their homes;
- to become acquainted when you call on families new to your congregation.

A PLAN FOR A FAMILY INTERVIEW (This plan requires approximately an hour to complete.)

Some Beginning Questions

1. What are the names, ages, and occupations of the members of your family?
2. Are you members of our congregation?
3. If so, when and how did you become members?
4. If not, how long have you been attending our church?
5. How has the church program helped your family?

Some Sentence Completions

1. Our family would feel affirmed in its strengths if . . . .
2. The church could help our family by . . . .
3. We wish the church would . . . .

Checklist

1. Ask family members to fill in the "Family Ministry Checklist" on page 43.
2. Review the completed checklist briefly to identify areas in which several family members indicated interest.

Conclusion

1. Ask family members if there is anything else they would like to say to you about themselves or the church or the kinds of family-ministry programs they would find helpful.
2. Thank each family member for participation and conclude the interview.

The important thing is to begin with a clear understanding of the needs of families in your congregation. Effective family ministry meets the real needs of real families.

FAMILY MINISTRY CHECKLIST

DIRECTIONS:

Check the box next to each item that describes something you want.
Then go back over the list and circle up to three items that are most
important to you.

GROWTH IN FAITH

I want to understand my growth in faith. ☐
I want to understand how children and youth grow in
    faith. ☐
I want information about how children and youth develop
        physically and mentally, ☐
        emotionally and socially, ☐
        morally. ☐
I want to know what the Bible teaches about family
    relationships. ☐

SEXUALITY

I want more information about human sexuality. ☐
I want help in teaching my children about sexuality. ☐

FAMILY RELATIONSHIPS

I want to learn ways my family can get along better. ☐
I want to learn communication skills in order to
        enrich my marriage, ☐
        strengthen my family. ☐
I want my family to learn how to
        plan family finances, ☐
        plan family fun and leisure, ☐
        make decisions better, ☐
        resolve conflicts, ☐
        plan education and careers, ☐
        plan for retirement, ☐
        plan for the care of an older relative. ☐
I want to learn how to work constructively with schools
    and teachers. ☐
I want to understand how peer groups, television,
    recreation programs, and organizations affect my family. ☐
I want to learn how to create and lead family and
    community organizations. ☐

gation, the next step in planning family ministry is to write objectives.

An objective is a statement of a target you want to hit. It is a statement of a change you want to make in an area of need. An objective is not a program idea but a statement of desired results. Writing objectives is a discipline that helps us focus on a specific change, result, or outcome we want to achieve.

We write objectives in order to clarify how we want to make a difference in relation to a need we have discovered. For example, a need we might have identified is that marriages need strengthening. An objective related to this area of need would target a specific aspect of marriage we wish to strengthen: communication skills, mutual and self-esteem, skills for negotiating conflict, or some other aspect.

An objective answers these questions: Who? What? When? and To what extent? In the following chart are some examples of areas of need and related statements of objectives.

NEED	SAMPLE OBJECTIVES
For young couples to enrich and strengthen their marriages.	To improve the communication skills of young married couples by mid-May.
For parents and teachers to understand the basics of child development.	To help mothers and fathers of infants and toddlers understand more about their children's behavior by the end of this fall.
For parents to take responsibility for the sex education of their children.	To help parents of children from birth to twelve years talk with their children about sexuality more often and more comfortably.

Objectives in family ministry generally will fall into three major areas:
- Those related to the need for more information.
- Those related to the need for "how-to" skills.
- Those related to the need for experiences to enrich family living.

3. DISCOVER RESOURCES

The next step in planning family ministry is to discover resources. The word *resources* means time, money, leadership, printed and audiovisual materials, and facilities. Two key questions are the following:

- Where do we find leadership?
- Where do we find printed and audiovisual materials?

Leadership

We have already alluded to sources of "expert" opinion in our discussion of identifying the needs of families. Some of these same persons may also be able to provide leadership for family-ministry events and programs. Among the persons who work with families are:

- The pastor of your church or another local church;
- A physician, psychologist, teacher, or experienced couple or parent in your own congregation;
- A guidance counselor or school psychologist;
- A staff person, usually a social worker or psychologist, from your local family service agency or mental health board;
- A community or parent educator from your local school;
- An adult educator from your local adult education program or community college;
- A college or university professor in the field of family studies;
- A staff person from Planned Parenthood, a crisis center, or a pastoral counseling center;
- A denominational Christian education worker for your area, state, or region.

An important strategy is to use the resources of your community in carrying out family-ministry programs. Besides providing competent leadership, this strategy has the added advantage of introducing families in your church to persons who may be helpful to them when they face a special need or crisis. Many such local leaders will be members of churches in your community and will be glad to be asked to apply their expertise in strengthening Christian families.

Printed and Audiovisual Materials

Information about printed and audiovisual resources is available from several places:

- Your regional or national denominational education staff will have lists of books and audiovisuals, information about available parent education programs, lists of denominational leaders in family ministry, and, often, a newsletter on family ministries.

- Most state libraries have films and other audiovisuals to lend; your local library will have a catalog.
- Your church may have access to an ecumenical media center.
- Your denomination's regional or national office may have a library of films and videotapes.

4. DEVELOP PROGRAM PLANS

With a clear statement of objectives and at least a preliminary idea about the resources available, you are ready to outline a program plan for fulfilling each objective you have set. You may want to develop several different kinds of programs:

- One-time events, such as a family retreat;
- Time-limited programs, such as a six-week class on parent-child communication;
- Longer term or ongoing programs, such as a support group for younger married couples.

To create a plan for a specific family-ministry program take these steps:

A. Begin with your objective statement. Clarify it by asking:

- Who are the specific persons and families we want to involve? What are their names?
- At the end of this program, in what ways will the participants be different? What new skills, changed attitudes, heightened motivation, or new concepts will the participants have acquired? List all the changes you hope for as a result of your program. Here are some examples:

  —Parents of toddlers who participate will be able to describe the developmental milestones typical of children between birth and age twelve.

  —Young marrieds who participate in the communication-skill training will be able to listen effectively to their partners; send clear messages about their own wants, feelings, thoughts, and behavior; and be able to use a three-step negotiation process for handling conflicts.

  —Families who participate in the financial-planning training will know the steps of budget construction, feel motivated to work out a budget for the coming year, and be ready to include the concept of percentage-giving to the church in their budget plan.

- When do we want the program to begin? end? How much time or how many sessions do we need?

B. Once you have clarified your objective, brainstorm all the ways you can think of to achieve it. For example, to enable parents to describe developmental milestones, you might:

- show a film on child development;
- invite a professor of psychology to lecture;
- visit a day-care center and observe children at different ages and stages;
- read and discuss a book on child development;
- ask a panel of experienced parents to describe the stages their children went through.

At this point, list *every* idea you can think of without worrying about how good each idea is.

C. Next, narrow the list of ideas to those that seem really workable. Arrange them in order or sequence. To test each possibility, ask: Why would I do that? How much would it help the participants? If you have identified a leader for the program this is a good time at which to involve the leader in planning with you.

D. Arrange your workable ideas into an overall design for the program.

- What do you need at the beginning to introduce people and ideas to one another?
- What activities will help develop the concepts, the skills, the motivations, and attitudes you want to achieve?
- Finally, what will help the program to end well?

E. Test your design by asking:

- How much time can be allotted to each part of the program?
- Are the kinds of activities varied so that interest will remain high among participants?
- Is there an element of surprise or joy or fun as well as seriousness and depth of thinking and sharing?
- What makes this program a Christian one? Does it draw on biblical insights and nourish the growth of participants' faith?

F. Now identify leaders and assign roles. It is crucial to name someone in the planning group as the coordinator (or implementor or overseer) of each particular program you plan to conduct. If the program calls for a leader team, spell out who will do what parts of the program.

A program plan can be a rough outline of objectives, times, places, and possible program ideas which you then hand to a leader for further development. Or it can be a detailed outline much like the session plan used by a church school teacher. A Family Ministry Program Plan Outline for guiding you through the planning process is on pages 49-50.

5. TEST PROGRAM PLANS

Test each of your program plans with potential participants and potential leaders. Check your plans against your budget and your calendar. This step will prevent future grief. No one likes to plan a program to which no one else comes! Testing your program plan involves several things.

- Go back to the potential participants whose needs you are seeking to meet and ask:
  - —Are we on target?
  - —What would make this program more helpful to you?
  - —Is the projected date a good one for you?
- Check with other groups of the church to see how your plans fit with theirs. This is a courteous thing to do and will give your program added visibility and attract support.
- In checking with potential leaders and in checking against budget and calendar, you may get early warning of potential difficulties. By testing your plans at this point, you still have time to revise them to accommodate the realities of budget, calendar, leadership, and most important, the felt needs of potential participants. Once you have tested your plan, you are ready to make final decisions and to implement them.

6. EVALUATE PROGRAM

After each family ministry program, evaluate it. This is an important way to collect information for future planning. How did participants feel about the program? Did they feel the objectives were achieved? What excited and rewarded them? What suggestions for a better experience do they have? You can seek evaluation of a program by asking participants to:

- fill in an evaluation form,
- write comments in response to questions on newsprint,
- be interviewed in person or by phone.

If your program was aimed at changing the way family members interact or behave, a follow-up interview six months later will help you see if the program made any lasting differences.

Evaluation by leaders is also important. It is probably worth the time for the planning group and the program leaders to meet

(continued on page 50)

FAMILY MINISTRY
PROGRAM PLAN OUTLINE

a. OBJECTIVE: _____
_____

WHO is to be helped or involved?

WHAT is to happen to participants? What new skills or changed attitudes or heightened motivations or new concepts will participants acquire? List what you hope will happen:

WHEN will this happen?

b. BRAINSTORM IDEAS. List all the ideas you have:

c. LIST THE MOST WORKABLE IDEAS:

    1. _____
    2. _____
    3. _____

d. PLACE IDEAS INTO A DESIGN:

- Beginning activities to introduce people and ideas to each other:

- Activities to develop concepts, skills, motivations, attitudes:

- Closing activities:
  (include evaluation)

together and discuss what went well and what did not go well and the changes in attitudes or motivations or skills that were seen. Review the participants' evaluations, and list learnings from this experience that you will want to apply to planning future events and programs.

Finally, you, the planners, need to evaluate each program and base your plans for the next phase in your family ministry on this foundation. Ask yourselves such questions as:

- Were the leaders effective?
- Was participation what we hoped for? Why? Why not?
- What program ideas worked well?
- What do we need to keep in mind for the next program?
- Did the program achieve the objective we set? To what extent?
- Do we need to work more on this objective or are we ready to move on to another?

CHAPTER 6

Toward a Comprehensive Family Ministry

In planning family ministry for your church, the most important information you can have is information about the felt needs and life situations of the specific families that are in your church. The whole point is to help the particular family units in your church and equip them for ministry. So, what follows here does not lessen the obligation of family-ministry planners to discover the actual needs of family members in their church and to identify the ways these families can be empowered for mission.

The program suggestions that are listed here are meant only to help you meet the needs of your congregation. If these suggestions correlate with the family needs and mission opportunities you have discovered, great! But *always* begin with the needs and opportunities of families in *your* church.

If family ministry is based on the actual needs of real families, and seeks to help real families fulfill their callings, then each church's approach to family ministry will be unique. No single approach to family ministry can possibly fit all churches. The emphasis in each congregation will reflect the particular families that belong to it. A comprehensive family ministry is one that responds to *all* the identified needs of the families who are involved. The outline offered here may help you to think about some areas of need or mission you have not explored. It may suggest a way to relate different parts of your family ministry to each other. It may help you to anticipate some program possibilities as the families within your congregation change and new ones join.

A word about settings for family ministry will be helpful at this point. Developing family ministry programs does not necessarily mean creating new program settings. Ongoing adult classes, regular gatherings of the church for community forums or church family nights, and established family camping experiences or retreats all provide opportunities for family ministry. Perhaps your congregation already sponsors a mothers' group, a men's fellowship, or programs of parent-child activities.

At the same time, new settings for family ministry may be helpful. You might want to consider support groups for persons in special life situations. A series of workshops to develop skills or explore particular issues may be an exciting departure for your congregation. Cosponsoring a conference on topics of interest to families with another church or with a family service agency is a possibility. Perhaps you might add some elective classes to your church school program focused on family issues, initiate some intergenerational events, or create one or more family clusters. Many of the program ideas suggested here can take place in settings which are traditional to your church as well as settings which are new.

One other word: Family education may well be happening in your community at the YWCA or YMCA, through the 4-H, or in the public schools or community college. The local cable television franchise may be interested in creating programs or showing films of help to families. A teaching church does not have to "do it all" or reinvent the wheel! If your community offers acceptable programs matching the needs of families in your congregation, by all means encourage participation in the community programs. Offer to cosponsor a family recreation program with the YWCA or YMCA or lend your church facility for a community college class on parenting.

The important thing is not that the church calendar be full, but that the needs of families be met! A useful role a task force in your church might play is to pull together in one list all that is happening for families in your community and to share that information with the community as a public service from your congregation. Such a list makes an excellent gift to leave with a new family in the neighborhood when someone from your church makes a call.

The suggestions for family ministry programs that follow are organized into the framework introduced in chapter 2, which includes three content areas and three skill areas.

CONTENT AREA #1: GROWTH IN FAITH

A. Learning about how persons grow in faith development can take place in a class setting. Parents are especially open to learning about the development of their children at three points:

- when their children are expected and "brand new,"

- when their children enter school, and
- when their children enter adolescence.

These "teachable moments" are good points at which to offer *courses in child development*.

B. A film series on faith development is another program possibility worth exploring. There are many excellent *films, plays, and television dramas* related to the saga of human growth.

C. Another way to nurture spiritual growth in adults and youth is through a *retreat* to explore their own faith journeys. In a retreat setting persons can:

- reflect on their own pilgrimages,
- share personal stories with one another, and
- be fed by input on appropriate Scripture with ample time for reflection.

A family camp or *family retreat* is an excellent occasion to help entire family units establish new patterns of family worship and communication about faith issues.

D. Youth and their middle-aged parents are both at critical points in their faith and life journeys.

- *Intergenerational events for youth and their parents* have significant value. Understanding one another's feelings about life now and hopes for the future can contribute to better communication between the generations and a deeper appreciation for one another.
- Other intergenerational groups that can help each other in their development are *young adults* and *middle adults*. Young adults are at a stage in life when relationships with mentors are especially helpful. Middle adults, those about half a generation older than the younger partner, are especially effective as mentors. Fostering mutually helpful relationships such as these is an important aspect of family ministry.

CONTENT AREA #2: SEXUALITY

A. Parents are the primary sexuality educators of children. *Courses for parents of young children in human sexuality* are probably the most helpful ministry the church can offer in this area of concern. Generally, parents have the greatest impact on their children's sexual values and behavior during the early years.

B. Parents often feel the greatest need for help in the area of sexuality when children reach adolescence. A particularly helpful way to approach sexuality education with families that include adolescents is through *intergenerational courses for parents and adolescents*. A retreat setting is especially helpful for this kind of experience.

C. Other areas to consider include:

- a course or seminar or retreat focused on *sexuality in the later years,*
- *peer-level courses* in sexuality education through the church school,
- a combination of *courses for parents and for children* running simultaneously or sequentially.

D. Human sexuality is an arena in which the church can provide an important ministry to the wider community.

- Consider sponsoring or cosponsoring (with a family counseling agency) a hot-line—a telephone number that can be called by youth who want accurate information or a sensitive listener.
- Distribute literature to places where parents or young people congregate.
- Other special areas of ministry might include support groups for victims of rape or incest, support groups for families dealing with the issue of homosexuality, and classes for persons with developmental disabilities and their families.

CONTENT AREA #3: FAMILY RELATIONSHIPS

A. There are many levels on which the church can foster a richer pattern of family relationships. At the level of the total congregation, *church family gatherings* are a way to enhance a sense of kinship and family relationship among all members of the church. Intergenerational celebrations can be a most significant form of family ministry.

B. Much is now known about the ingredients of healthy family relationships, and a *course for parents and youth on what makes a healthy family* is a possibility to explore. At the heart of such a course is the concept of the family system. This concept helps each person see the family as a whole unit and see how her or his place and role within the family affects all the other members.

C. *Family clusters* are an important strategy for fostering stronger families. A concept developed by Margaret Sawin, the family cluster is a gathering of four to six family units who contract to meet for a period of weeks with a skilled leader. The agenda of the cluster is derived from the interests and needs of the participants, and the focus is on enriching the quality of life in the participating family units.

D. Another approach to intergenerational family building that many churches have found helpful is *"adopt a grandparent" programs.* Young families who are living at some distance from their older kin and older persons or couples who are separated from younger family can be matched for their mutual growth and enjoyment. Family-ministry planners in this instance are focusing on helping the human relationship to occur rather than on structuring a particular event.

E. *Marriage enrichment* is one of the most widely known and thoroughly tested programs for strengthening family units. Marriage is the center around which the whole family system is built. Helping that relationship to flourish ought to be a major focus of family ministry. Marriage enrichment events are especially helpful at several specific points in the life of a couple:

- during the first year of marriage, especially about halfway through that first year;
- when children arrive and changes associated with that adjustment occur;
- during the empty nest period, when a couple faces retirement and preparation for old age.

At the same time, throughout the years regular opportunities for the couple to learn and grow with each other are very important. Ongoing groups or classes for couples are significant ways that a church can minister to marriages.

F. Parenting and the parent-child relationship combine as another focus for family ministry.

- A couples' class provides an excellent setting for courses on the meaning of Christian parenthood, discipline, or other issues.
- Remember—church-related parents are not alone in their work of raising children! Of enduring concern to parents *and to other adults also* is the sharing of Christian values with children. Workshops, support groups, and retreats built around such themes as parenting for peace and justice, care for the earth, and how to relate with persons of different cultures and ethnic backgrounds are helpful experiences for parents and all adults who care about children.

G. Another area of family ministry involves *support groups for persons in transitional situations.* Consider forming support groups for single parents, for parents with developmentally disabled children, for women making a transition from full-time homemaking to paid employment (either by choice or because of divorce or the death of a spouse), or for recently widowed persons. Such groups will probably need to be sponsored by more than one congregation.

SKILL AREA #1: COMMUNICATION SKILLS

Communication is *the* basic skill that families need.

A. *Courses in couple communication* are the foundational program offerings. One excellent program of proven success is offered by Interpersonal Communication, Inc. It is a four-week, twelve-hour course in how to communicate better and build couple esteem in the process. For information write Interpersonal Communication, Inc. at the address listed in the Recommended Resources.

B. *Courses in parent-child communication* are important as well and can be built into an ongoing class or can be the focus of a conference or retreat. Some groups offering courses or packaged programs for parents are listed in the Recommended Resources along with resources on communication for adult church school classes.

C. *Intergenerational experiences that help families talk about faith* is another kind of program to consider. *General communication skills* can be taught to children, youth, and adults in intergenerational settings as well.

D. Some churches have found that *assertiveness training,* especially for women, contributes to healthier communication patterns in families.

SKILL AREA #2: PLANNING SKILLS

A. *Seminars in family financial planning and stewardship* are an important part of a family ministry program. Families with older children can benefit from intergenerational experiences in which planning skills are taught, and opportunities for education in values formation are also included.

B. *Methods for decision making, negotiating conflicts, and problem solving* are important skill areas that can be dealt with in a family cluster, a family camp, or a short-term intergenerational course.

C. *Life-planning skills* are another important skill area to consider. Many persons faced with the need to change occupation or to move into paid employment from homemaking have found life-planning workshops helpful.

- The format of the life-planning workshop has much to offer couples who are committed to enriching their marriages and to developing their individual careers in relationship to one another.
- Life-planning workshops can also be structured intergenerationally as an opportunity for youth and parents to help one another take steps in career development.

D. Another issue facing increasing numbers of families is *planning for the care of older family members.* A workshop on this topic can help families anticipate how they will respond to illness and disability among grandparents, uncles, aunts, and others.

SKILL AREA #3: ORGANIZATIONAL SKILLS

Family ministry is concerned not only with the inner dynamics of family units but also with the ways in which family units interact with the institutions of the community.

A. *Family-school relationships* are an important area of concern.

- *A workshop for parents and teachers on how to build a mutually supportive relationship* is one example of a family-ministry program aimed at helping families relate better to schooling institutions.
- *A forum on values education for parents and other interested community members* could explore how the roles of family, church, and schools might contribute to better home-school relations in your community.
- Consider *a forum or conference on the parental role in guiding public education*.

B. Parents of children with disabilities have long worked at teaching themselves how to be effective advocates for their children, but all parents at various times need to play the role of advocate. A course or workshop on *how to be an advocate for your child* might be offered to both parents and workers with children and youth in the church. Leaders from such organizations as Association for Retarded Citizens or a citizen advocacy organization could help you with such a project.

C. Another approach to enhancing organizing skills among families is to create *action groups*.

- One group might monitor meetings of the public school board of education, a day-care center, or community recreational groups such as the Little League, and share observations in a newsletter or radio/TV commentary.
- Another group might focus on juvenile justice. Building relationships with the officers of the juvenile court, the members of the probation department, or those who administer shelters for runaways are important avenues for increasing our awareness about family systems that have broken down for one reason or another.
- A third group of families might be ready to become "interim families" for those who need a temporary home away from home. Interim families take in a young person, for a night or a week, who needs a temporary place to live until a court acts, a parent is released, or some other difficulty is resolved.

D. Persons who are professional trainers of foster parents can be enlisted to help interested nonparents in the congregation learn *how to be parent surrogates*. Parent surrogates can offer "respite care" to young parents who cannot easily afford a baby-sitter for a weekend away (for instance, while they attend the marriage enrichment event!). Check with your local family service agency to obtain such persons.

E. Much that is good in church life, from growth in numbers of church members to helping the community be a healthier place for families, occurs because family units know how to reach out to other family units. A workshop, retreat, or cluster on *family-to-family faith sharing* can increase the number of skilled family members who are ready to reach out to others and include them in the church or recruit them to the cause of better schools, renewed neighborhoods, or new recreational programs.

POSTCRIPT AND ONE
LAST QUESTION

It is clear from the 1980 census that during this decade we will be more aware of families and family issues. More older persons will need to decide whether to maintain their own homes, live with another, or move in with family members. There will be more parents of young children as the "baby-boom" generation moves through the child-rearing years. Already some day-care centers and nursery schools are showing significant increases in attendance. More women will be working outside of the home and causing their family systems to change. More couples will be seeking richer marriages as the value of committed relationships becomes more apparent. More family units will be seeking help to achieve greater satisfaction in family life as the possibilities for materialistic escape diminish in a world of economic constraint. A new appreciation of the family as the primary educator of children is emerging in this decade and will stimulate broad reassessments of how the next generation is to be educated. Certainly families with a Christian orientation will be looking for ways to make their witness and to make a difference in their neighborhoods and in the nation. We can anticipate that increasing attention will be paid to family life and that individual expectation of family life will probably increase in the eighties.

The church remains as the one institution where entire family units are present together and where the whole range of experiences across the life cycle are available for reflection, exploration, and celebration. The church harbors a vision of justice and wholeness which can empower families to be centers of blessing and health for all those around them. When the community comes to the church asking us to help families fulfill their potential and their responsibilities to the next generation, will we be ready?

RECOMMENDED RESOURCES FOR FAMILY MINISTRY

FAITH DEVELOPMENT

Bringing up Children in the Christian Faith, John H. Westerhoff, III, Winston, 1980.

Christian Child Development, Iris V. Cully, Harper and Row, 1979.

Stages of Faith, James W. Fowler, Harper and Row, 1981.

Helping Your Child Discover Faith, Delia Touchton Halverson, Judson, 1982.

SEXUALITY

"A Family Talks About Sex," half-hour color film. Order from denominational media center or from Perennial Education, Inc., 477 Roger Williams, P.O. Box 8555, Ravinia, Highland Park, IL 60035.

Embodiment: An Approach to Sexuality and Christian Theology, James B. Nelson, Augsburg, 1979.

The Family Book About Sexuality, Mary S. Calderone and Eric W. Johnson, Harper and Row, 1981.

God Made Us: About Sex and Growing Up, Graded Press, The United Methodist Publishing House, 201 8th Avenue, S. Nashville, TN 37202. A course for parents, church school teachers, and older elementary children.

Man as Male and Female, Paul K. Jewett, Eerdmans, 1975.

Parents of the Homosexual, David K. Switzer and Shirley A. Switzer, Westminster, 1980.

FAMILY RELATIONSHIPS AND COMMUNICATION

Association of Couples for Marriage Enrichment, 459 S. Church Street, P.O. Box 10596, Winston Salem, NC 27108. International voluntary organization of married couples trains and certifies marriage-enrichment leaders.

Black Families and the Struggle for Survival, Andrew Billingsley, Friendship, 1974.

Christian Education in Family Clusters, Mel Williams and Mary Ann Brittain, Judson, 1982.

Church Family Gatherings, Joe Leonard, Jr., ed., Judson, 1978.

Expecting, Elizabeth Hambrick-Stowe, Judson, 1979.

Family Enrichment with Family Clusters, Margaret M. Sawin, Judson, 1979.

Friends, Partners, and Lovers, Warren L. Molton, Judson, 1979.

Love and Negotiate, John Scanzoni, Word, 1979.

Nursery Packets, Judson/Bethany, 1980
  - "This Child of Ours," for parents expecting their first child.
  - "Our Growing Family," for children and parents awaiting a new baby.

Parent Effectiveness Training, Effectiveness Training Associates, 110 S. Euclid Avenue, Pasadena, CA 91101. For information about P.E.T. programs.

Preparing for Christian Marriage, Joan and Richard Hunt (couples' edition); *Preparing for Christian Marriage,* Antoinette and Leon Smith (pastors' edition), Abingdon, 1982.

Systematic Training for Effective Parenting, American Guidance Service, Inc., Circle Pines, MN 55014.

Interpersonal Communication, Inc., 300 Clifton Avenue at the Carriage House, Minneapolis, MN 55403 offers courses, materials, leader training in couple communication and family enrichment.

Putting the Pieces Together, Carter and Leavenworth, Judson, 1977. Available, in both participants' and leaders' editions, for church-related single parents' support groups.

Young Black Adults: Liberation and Family Attitudes, George B. Thomas, Friendship, 1974.

FAMILIES AND SOCIETY

All Our Children: The American Family Under Pressure, Kenneth Keniston and the Carnegie Council on Children, Harcourt, Brace, Jovanovich, 1977.

The Christian and the Public Schools, George Van Alstine, Abingdon, 1982.

The Public School and the Family, Hope Leichter. One of a series of monographs with study guide. For information, write United Ministries in Education, % Educational Ministries, Valley Forge, PA 19481.

Parenting for Peace and Justice, Kathleen and James McGinnis, Orbis, 1981.